More Praise for EVERYONE HAS THE RIGHT TO MY OPINION

"To achieve the Pulitzer Prize in one's lifetime is no small feat. For Michael Ramirez to earn *two* Pulitzers puts his editorial cartoons and analyses in a league of their own. In the following pages of *Everyone Has the Right to My Opinion*, it's immediately evident why Michael's legacy will be as one of the greatest editorial cartoonists of our time. We're proud to provide the platform for Michael's great work in the pages of *Investor's Business Daily*."

> **—William J. O'Neil**
> **Chairman and Founder, *Investor's Business Daily* and Investors.com**

"Who said you can't be conservative and funny at the same time? I found myself laughing and nodding my head. Michael Ramirez, one of America's great political cartoonists, packs a real wallop."

> **—Robert D. Novak**
> **Nationally syndicated columnist**

"Mike Ramirez's pen is a weapon of mass destruction: lethal, explosive, and always on target. From Hollywood to Washington to Iran, no blowhard is safe. No sacred cow is immune. A picture may be worth 1,000 words. This collection of Ramirez's finest work: Priceless."

> **—Michelle Malkin**
> **Author of *Unhinged: Exposing Liberals Gone Wild*
> Fox News contributor**

"Michael Ramirez's cartoons brilliantly expose the results of centralized tyranny and ignorance."

> **—Walter E. Williams**
> **Professor of Economics, George Mason University, and nationally syndicated columnist**

"Michael Ramirez is very, very funny. You may not agree with him — I usually don't — but I dare you not to laugh!"

> **—Susan Estrich**
> **Professor of Law and Political Science, USC Gould School of Law
> Fox News Analyst**

"Insightful, impactful, frighteningly beautiful, and often hilarious political commentary on our world. Ramirez's editorial cartoons would always be funny if the punchline weren't so often very sad."

> **—Arthur B. Laffer**

"One Michael Ramirez cartoon is worth far more than a thousand editorials. Heaven help the publicly pompous, fraudulent or incompetent butts of his brilliant, wickedly witty pen. Ramirez is an unsparingly perceptive, accurate and funny ethicist. His hilarious cartoons are heat-seeking missiles. Not even the most artful political dodgers can escape."

> **—Pete Wilson**
> **Governor of California, 1991–1999**

"Michael Ramirez gives new meaning to the phrase "drawn and quartered." Rather than be depicted in a Ramirez cartoon, most politicians would choose to be chopped into fourths and disemboweled. (They don't have a lot of guts anyway.) Being literally drawn and quartered means pols could run for office in four different electoral districts at once. Being drawn by Ramirez means they're really done for."

—**P.J. O'Rourke**
Journalist, Author

"Michael's incredible talent is demonstrated by his consistent ability to capture the moment in a historic perspective."

—**Don Sundquist**
Governor of Tennessee, 1995–2003

"Two Pulitzer prizes don't begin to describe Michael Ramirez's talent for portraying the essence of an idea in a single image. In his case, one picture is worth a thousand Pulitzers. He is a national treasure, and this anthology of his work is our way to share in it."

—**Christopher Cox**
Chairman of the United States Securities and Exchange Commission

EVERYONE HAS THE RIGHT TO MY OPINION

EVERYONE HAS THE RIGHT TO MY OPINION

MICHAEL RAMIREZ

Foreword by Dr. William J. Bennett

WILEY

John Wiley & Sons, Inc.

Published by John Wiley & Sons, Inc., Hoboken, New Jersey.
Published simultaneously in Canada.

For general information on our other products and services or for technical support, please contact our Customer Care Department within the United States at (800) 762-2974, outside the United States at (317) 572-3993 or fax (317) 572-4002.

Wiley also publishes its books in a variety of electronic formats. Some content that appears in print may not be available in electronic books. For more information about Wiley products, visit our web site at www.wiley.com.

Library of Congress Cataloging-in-Publication Data:
Ramirez, Michael.
  Everyone has the right to my opinion: Investor's Business Daily's Pulitzer prize-winning cartoonist/Michael Ramirez.
    p. cm.
  Includes index.
    1. American wit and humor, Pictorial. 2. Editorial cartoons—United States. I. Title.
  NC1429.R28A4 2008
  741.5'6973—dc22

                                                          2008033886

ISBN 978-0-470-40677-9

Printed in the United States of America

10 9 8 7 6 5 4 3 2 1

To my parents, Fumiko and I. Edward Ramirez, to the entire Ramirez family, to Deborah McNeely, and to our valiant troops around the world whose courage and sacrifice secure our freedom and liberty.

It is the mark of an educated mind to be able to entertain a thought without accepting it.

—Aristotle

CONTENTS

FOREWORD

Politics is among the most noble of human activities, but we are at risk of forgetting that today. Too many people have embraced a view that is best described as cynical: They assume that politics consists of nothing but greedy grabs for power, power being the end, politics the means. So long as men are not angels, there always will be selfish and dishonest politicians, to be sure. But politics also offers a stage for great acts of human excellence. Politics illuminates courage, moderation, prudence, and justice. It is where magnanimity shines most brightly. Why else would the great William Shakespeare choose political settings for his greatest plays?

An exercise in ruling and being ruled in turn, politics happens when men and women deliberate, debate, and sometimes fight about who is going to rule, who is going to get ruled, and what kind of rule will be enforced and obeyed. Politics, in other words, is made possible by and cultivates *logos*, the Greek word that means both articulate speech and reason. At its core, politics is *the* human activity: men and women coming together to think, speak, articulate, and improve their understanding of the true, the good, and the just, as they attempt to enshrine these qualities into the public laws.

Some might find the following suggestion controversial, but I assume readers enjoy a taste of controversy lest they would not have in their hands this book, which is filled with controversy: In order to live life to its fullest capacity, human beings must be self-governing; the problem is that self-government is a rare and therefore precious phenomenon in human history. Most human beings throughout most of history have not participated in their own political rule; instead, they have been lorded over without their consent, forced to live a kind of life not of their choosing. They were deprived of the opportunity to lead and enjoy a fuller life, the life of a self-governing human being.

We Americans are blessed to find ourselves as the beneficiaries of the greatest experiment in self-government, what Abraham Lincoln called "the last best hope of earth." But let us not be naive. It is nowhere foreordained that American self-government and freedom will survive forever. Even the Founders were unsure of that.

Enter the world of editorial cartooning. The editorial cartoon stands alone as the most succinct of all forms of politics. Within only several square inches on a piece of paper, a good editorial cartoon, sometimes without including one word, is like a jolt of adrenaline through the veins of a political people. By their very nature, editorial cartoons stir controversy, spark debate and discussion, and move minds to think thoughts not thought before. The art of the editorial cartoon has been transformed over centuries, and perfected in certain ways, but it remains a political art just as it was at the time of our nation's founding.

Those cartoons, then, and the best of them today, encourage people to be feisty and to think for themselves, which is why so many of us take to, enjoy, and circulate editorial cartoons. Newspaper-reading Americans consistently rank the editorial cartoon as their favorite part of the newspaper. That is good news. It means the political spirit of freedom is still alive in America.

Enter Michael Ramirez. If the editorial cartoon stands as the most succinct of all political art forms, then Michael Ramirez stands as the master artist. Previously at the *Los Angeles Times* and now at *Investor's Business Daily*, Michael has taken the art of editorial cartooning to heights not seen before. The Pulitzer Prize committee agreed not once, but twice. His drawings are sometimes sad, sometimes uplifting, but often just downright funny, and they always are provocative. It is not his pencil, however, that makes Michael special, or maybe even dangerous—it is the genius that moves his pencil.

When one studies Michael's cartoons, one is watching a rare combination of artful genius, intellect, and imagination moving together in harmony from mind to hand to paper, allowing others to enter the world of Michael Ramirez and wrestle with the same problems and questions with which he is wrestling. Studying Michael's cartoons is an intensely public and political exercise, and thus a good thing for the country.

Michael Ramirez is among the foremost artists and most astute political commentators of our time. He is a patriot as well. He cannot hide his love for this wonderful country because of what he is: a political man who uses his extraordinary gift to promote reflection, debate, and discussion about the most important questions we face as a nation. He is a political man who draws cartoons, and he uses those cartoons to help us become more political. He is, in his unique way, recovering the political conditions necessary for self-government. He is helping us to live the fully human lives we are capable of living. He is a national treasure, and his country should thank him. I know I do.

—**Dr. William J. Bennett**

ACKNOWLEDGMENTS

A first book is an exciting but enormous undertaking. Many people encouraged me and helped me to put this book together. I thank my mother and father, who have been supportive of me in all my endeavors. I have been blessed with the best parents and the best family in the world: my brother Ed, his wife Jane, and their daughter Julia; my sister Victoria, her husband Denley, and their brand-new daughter Alexandra; my brother Alexander, his wife Lori, and their daughters Ke'ea and Ellie; my sister Liz, her husband Bryan, their son Bryson, their daughter Amelie, and Bryan's brother Hannibal. I thank my girlfriend Deborah for her sage advice, her wisdom and hard work, and her infinite patience (especially her infinite patience).

There were so many people who were generous with their time and made significant contributions to the book. Among them: George Will, Rush Limbaugh, Robert Novak, Bill O'Reilly, Governor Mike Huckabee, Larry Kudlow, Michelle Malkin, Susan Estrich, P.J. O'Rourke, Walter Williams, Art Laffer, Grover Norquist, and my dear friends, Governor Pete Wilson, Governor Don Sundquist, and Ann Coulter.

I would like to thank Dr. William J. Bennett for his generosity of time and for being my hero.

I thank the friends without whom I could not have finished this project so quickly: my friend Ray Gonzales, who has been talking politics with me every Tuesday for over 20 years; my friend Mark Joseph, who is my spiritual ally; and my dear friends, Stan and Hunter Freeberg, who are part of my extended family. Stan is a national treasure and a satirical genius, and Hunter is his equal. I thank Chip Saltsman and Paul and Angie Shanklin for their friendship and for always trying to give me bad ideas for cartoons. I thank Duane Doherty and Linda Breakstone for their moral support.

I would also like to thank my friends Claremont President Brian Kennedy and Tom Karako, and acknowledge all my comrades at the Claremont Institute. I thank my dear friend Tom Krannawitter for his profundity and prose, and for being my ace reliever in the clutch.

I would like to thank my good friend SEC Chairman Christopher Cox for all of his encouragement through the years.

Special thanks to William J. O'Neil for being a true visionary in the newspaper industry, who is going against the national trend and investing in his paper, expanding its content and hiring the best and the brightest. It is what makes *Investor's Business Daily* unique and its editorial page the best in the country.

I want to thank my good friend Kathleen Sherman for her insight and advice and for making this book possible. I want to thank *IBD* editor Wes Mann, and my colleagues Terry Jones, Kerry Jackson, Monica Showalter, Tom McArdle, Matt Galgani, along with the rest of the staff at *Investor's Business Daily*. You are so bright, and I am proud to be part of the team at *IBD*.

I want to thank Rick Newcombe for his friendship, his counsel, and all his help. I look forward to my new relationship with Creators Syndicate.

No journalist can have an impact without having his work distributed to the world. I thank Glenda Winders for her friendship and support. I want to thank my colleagues at Copley News Service for all of their hard work over the years, ensuring that I receive hate mail from the farthest recesses of the world.

I would like to acknowledge my friends and former colleagues at the *Los Angeles Times*, the *Memphis Commercial Appeal*, and *USA Today*.

Thanks to my editor, Pamela Van Giessen, and her assistant, Kate Wood, at John Wiley & Sons for finally forcing me to put it all in a book and making it appear that I am far more literate than I really am.

I thank God for all the blessings in my life.

And last but not least, I want to thank all the politicians. I couldn't have done it without you.

INTRODUCTION

It's a calm morning; a rectangle of light shimmers from the dawn through the window and across my drawing board. The newspapers have been read, the blogs scanned, and the television is reverberating with the latest news. It's an election year and the rhetorical winds of change are blowing again, and my pen is poised and ready to attack. And I'm stuck here writing an Introduction to my book instead of leaping into the political fray.

I'm an editorial cartoonist. I'm not a writer. If I could write I would be a columnist.

My publisher wanted me to recount stories like the time I won my first Pulitzer Prize and I was greeted at the awards ceremony at Columbia University by an enormous protest. Several protestors approached our car. I realized they had no idea what I looked like when they handed me a flyer protesting myself. So I joined the picket line. I may be the only Pulitzer Prize winner who has protested himself.

Or the time I was investigated by the Secret Service over one of my cartoons.

Or the time I was in Havana interviewing the Minister of Information. He refused to answer questions about imprisoned journalists, censorship, the Brothers in Arms flight that was shot down in international airspace, or the tugboat full of Cuban refugees that was capsized outside of Havana Harbor, drowning most of its occupants.

I brought up the elaborate political process Cuban journalists had to go through to get into print. I brought up the fact Cuban editorial cartoonists could not draw cartoons of Fidel or Che Guevara. I told him that in the United States we believe a country that cannot make fun of its leaders is usually a country imprisoned by its leaders. I asked him one last question, the camera zooming in on his face: "What is your favorite Fidel Castro joke?" His face went ashen. He was speechless. And I got my answer.

It was the same answer William M. Tweed and Tammany Hall gave 120 years earlier in reaction to Thomas Nast's cartoons. Boss Tweed was a little more vociferous in his condemnation, "Stop them damn pictures. I don't care so much what the papers say about me. My constituents don't know how to read, but they can't help seeing them damned pictures!" It was clear the Castro regime recognized the power of the pen.

Confucius believed only the virtuous should exercise power. Aristotle argued that only by participating in politics can one truly live an ethical life. Machiavelli altered that thinking. He believed the stable state was more important than virtue. John Locke believed that man had certain "natural rights." Rousseau believed man was free but subject to *volonté générale* or the general will. But what defines the general will? And what instrument of governance would determine the general will?

In the Declaration of Independence Thomas Jefferson wrote, "We hold these truths to be self-evident, that all men are created equal, that they are endowed by their Creator with certain unalienable Rights, that among these are Life, Liberty and the pursuit of Happiness." But while these rights are indeed endowed by a creator and guaranteed by our Constitution, it is government that upholds these liberties and it is men who constitute the government.

There are those who believe the Constitution is merely a starting point for negotiation. James Madison wrote, "I believe there are more instances of the abridgement of freedom of the people by gradual and silent encroachments by those in power than by violent and sudden usurpations."

Editorial cartoons are a check to the erosion of our liberties and a first line of defense against the advance of the unrestrained power of government. One good editorial cartoon can have a significant impact on the political dialogue of the day. If done well, it can influence those who govern to govern responsibly, and expose them when they do not.

Albert Einstein once said, "Two things are infinite: the universe and human stupidity; and I'm not sure about the universe." Einstein was right. It is this axiom that makes political cartooning important. The people who ultimately govern will make mistakes. They are human, after all. But history has demonstrated that power can turn leaders into monsters. Editorial cartoonists will gladly point out the shortcomings of the powerful in an effort to keep them human.

And while it is quite remarkable that cartoons can have such an impact, it is equally remarkable and shortsighted that newspapers, in their infinite wisdom, are relinquishing this influence and abandoning the position of editorial cartoonist. H.L. Mencken once said, "Give me a good cartoonist and I can throw out half the editorial staff." Poll after poll has demonstrated that, for the people who read the editorial page, the editorial cartoon continues to be the most popular feature on the page.

Part of the damage is self-inflicted. Where the modern trend in editorial cartooning has been to make simple jokes about current affairs, humor without a substantive statement diminishes the importance of the editorial cartoon. Editorial cartoonists who don't take their jobs seriously should not expect to be taken seriously.

An editorial cartoon is not just a funny picture. An editorial cartoon is a fine instrument of journalism. At times it is sharp and refined, its message cutting quickly to the point; at times, blunt, with its dark imagery seizing the readers' attention.

As with any editorial, the cartoon has a point. It tells a story. It defines an issue. It challenges hypocrisy. It reveals the best and the worst of humanity. It calls the reader to arms against the complacent, the lethargic, the evildoers, the indolent body politic, and the champions of the status quo. It exposes the assorted predators of society.

An editorial cartoon is not humorous for the sake of humor. It is not controversial for the sake of controversy. It is neither conservative nor liberal. Whether you agree with it philosophically or not, a good editorial cartoon engages the reader in debate. It informs and challenges. It draws the reader into the democratic process.

This book is a compilation of over 20 years of editorial cartooning. You can literally follow history as it weaves its way through my cartoons from the black-and-white era of the early years at the *Memphis Commercial Appeal* and *USA Today* and the *Los Angeles Times* to the full-color pages of *Investor's Business Daily*.

Some of my cartoons may make you laugh. Some of my cartoons will make you cringe. But all of them, I hope, will make you think. As you view my editorial cartoons, I hope you can see the messages intricately woven into each design, always revealing a strong point of view.

But enough of this; in short, it's a book about pictures.

EVERYONE HAS THE RIGHT TO MY OPINION

THE 2008 PULITZER COLLECTION

One of the great things about books is sometimes there are some fantastic pictures.

—George W. Bush

~3~

"AS A MATTER OF FACT, WE JUST BOUGHT ANOTHER SUV...."

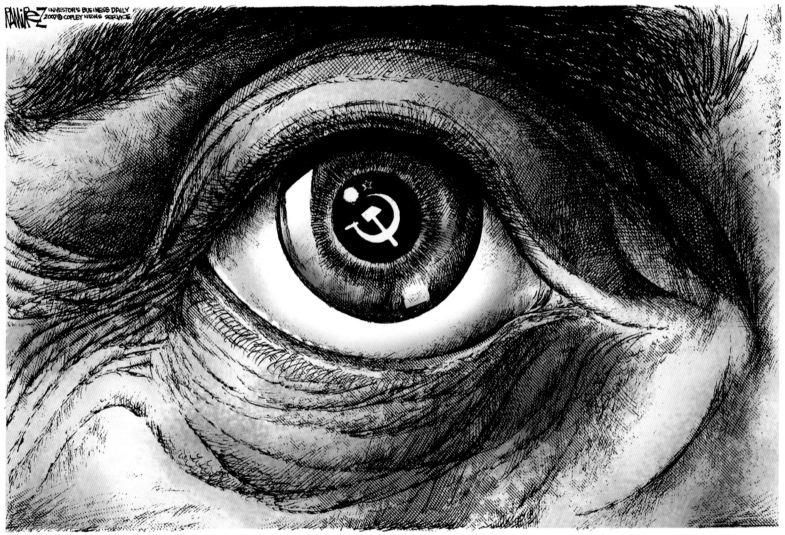

I LOOKED THE MAN IN THE EYE. I WAS ABLE TO GET A SENSE OF HIS SOUL. – BUSH ON PUTIN

THE GREAT WALL

THE ANCHOR

"THAT'S LOW ENOUGH."

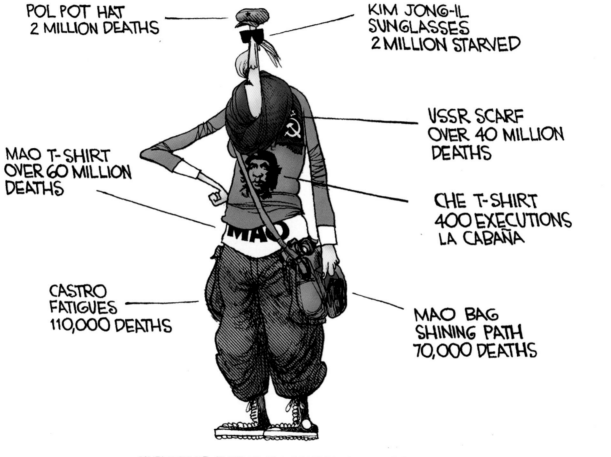

POL POT HAT
2 MILLION DEATHS

KIM JONG-IL
SUNGLASSES
2 MILLION STARVED

USSR SCARF
OVER 40 MILLION
DEATHS

MAO T-SHIRT
OVER 60 MILLION
DEATHS

CHE T-SHIRT
400 EXECUTIONS
LA CABAÑA

CASTRO
FATIGUES
110,000 DEATHS

MAO BAG
SHINING PATH
70,000 DEATHS

FASHIONS FOR THE IGNORANT CELEBRITY

RAMIREZ INVESTOR'S BUSINESS DAILY 2007© COPLEY NEWS SERVICE

www.IBDeditorials.com/cartoons

~19~

~22~

MORAL VALUES

If it were not for the reporters, I would tell you the truth.

—Chester A. Arthur

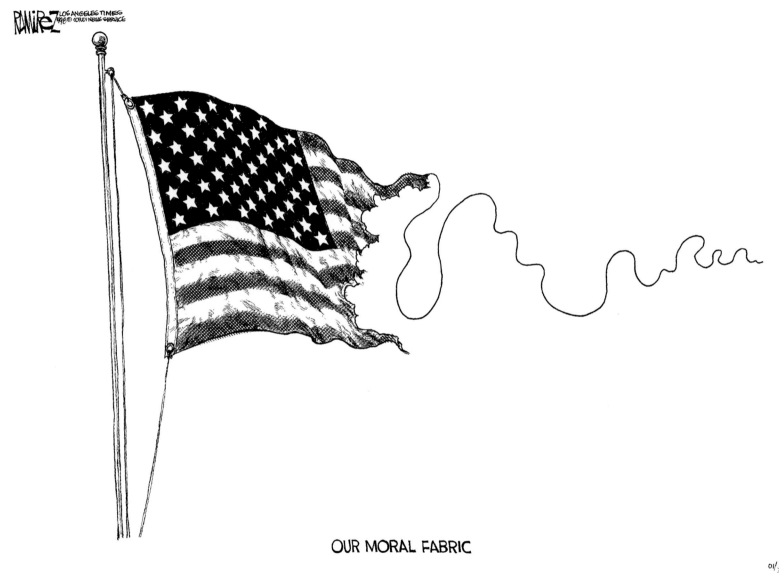

OUR MORAL FABRIC

01/29

New York Governor Eliot Spitzer

~32~

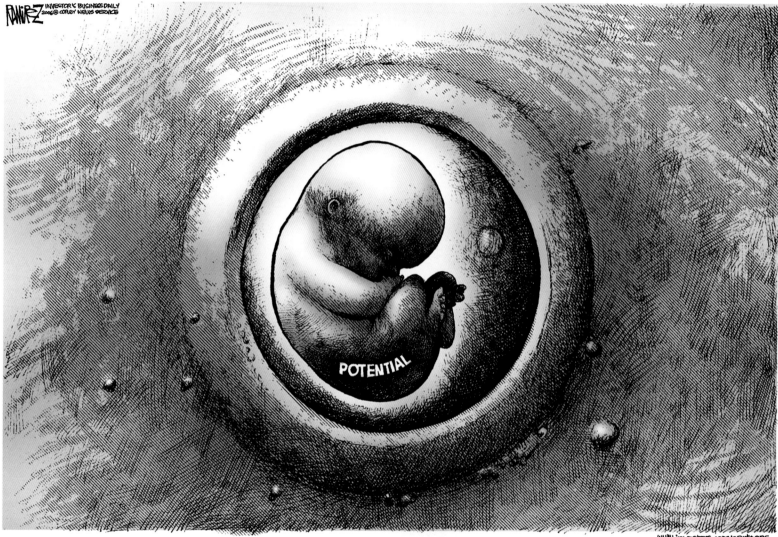

WHAT IS IN EVERY HUMAN EMBRYO

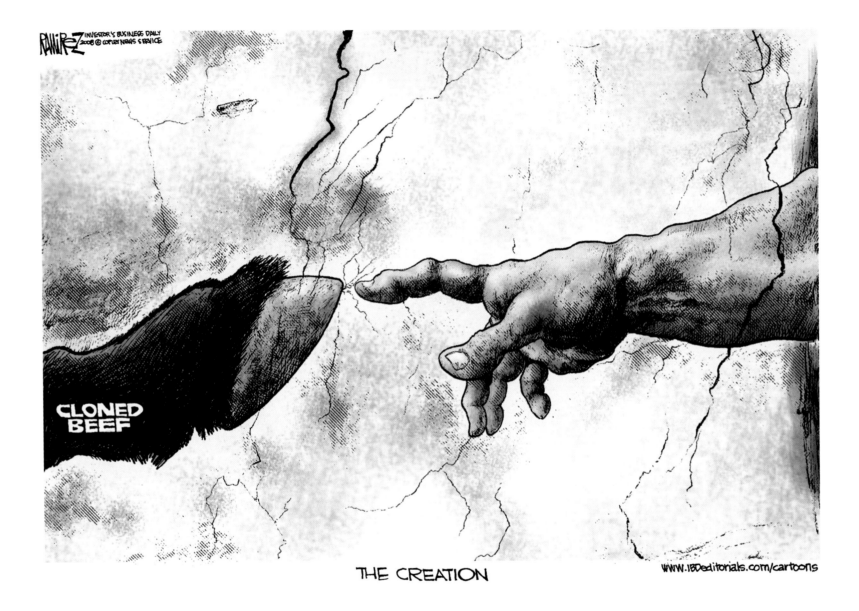

THE CREATION

HOLLYWOOD

You can fool all of the people some of the time, and some of the people all of the time, but you can not fool all of the people all of the time.

—Abraham Lincoln

~38~

~39~

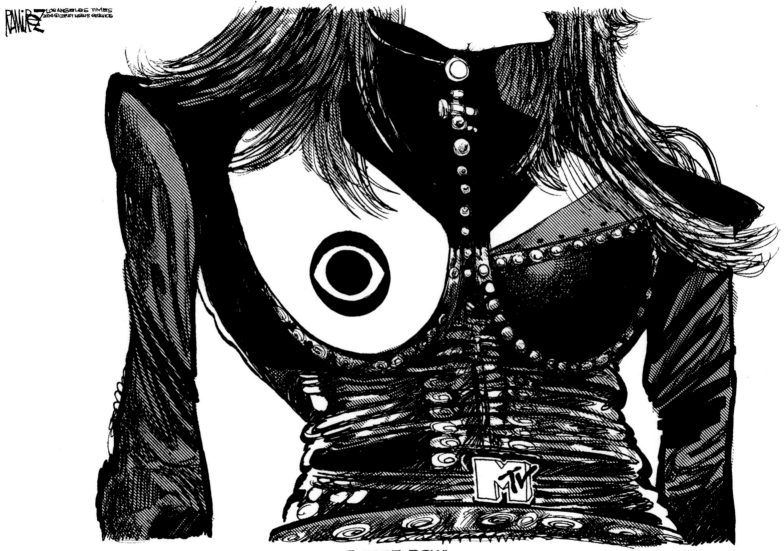

SLEAZE BOWL

NEA Self Portrait   *with apologies to Mr. Rockwell.

~47~

GORE'S CARBON FOOTPRINT

www.IBDeditorials.com/cartoons

~49~

www.investors.com/cartoons

DOMESTIC AFFAIRS

A government big enough to give you everything you want is a government big enough to take from you everything you have.

—Gerald R. Ford

MARLBORO COUNTRY

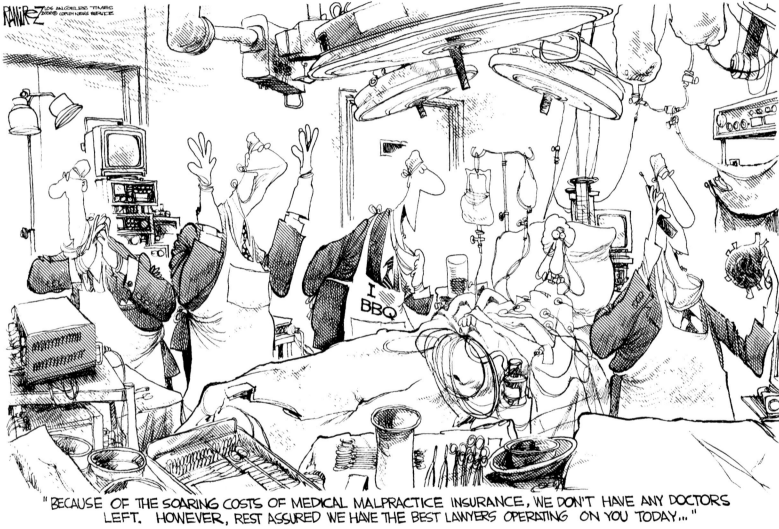

"BECAUSE OF THE SOARING COSTS OF MEDICAL MALPRACTICE INSURANCE, WE DON'T HAVE ANY DOCTORS LEFT. HOWEVER, REST ASSURED WE HAVE THE BEST LAWYERS OPERATING ON YOU TODAY..."

~58~

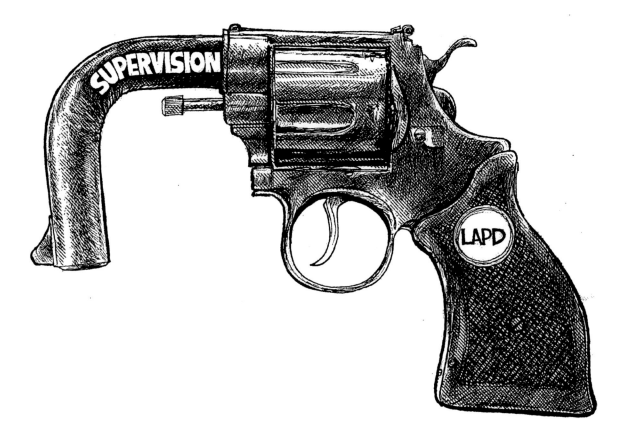

AFFIRMATIVE
ACTION

THE SEDUCTION OF THE EPISCOPAL CHURCH

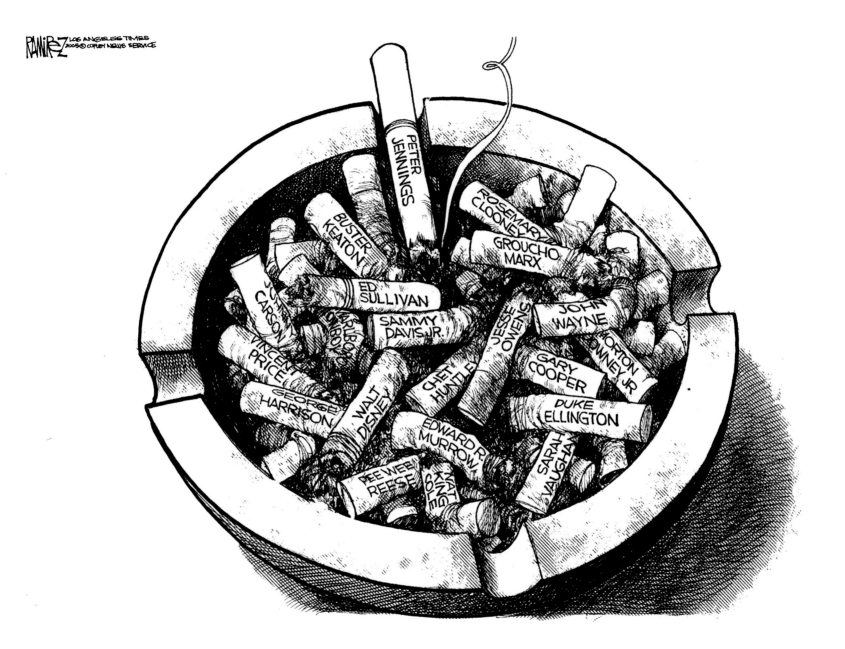

POINTING FINGERS ARE NOT HELPING HANDS....

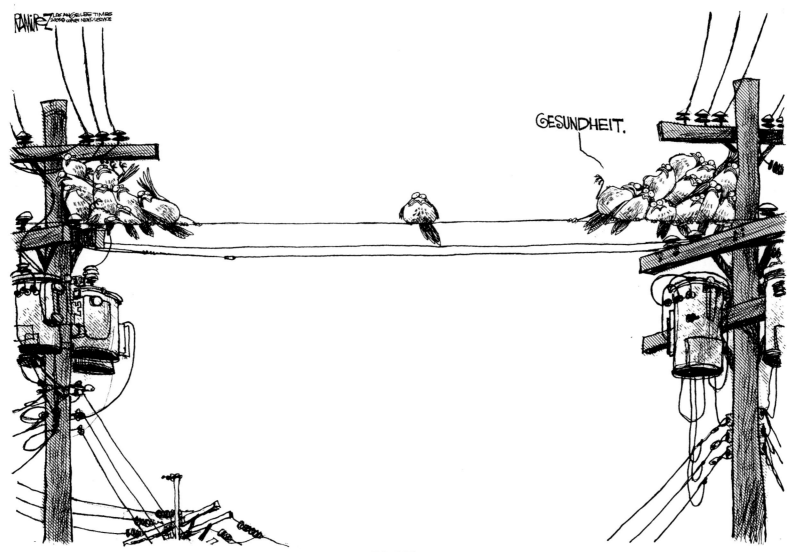

Bird Flu

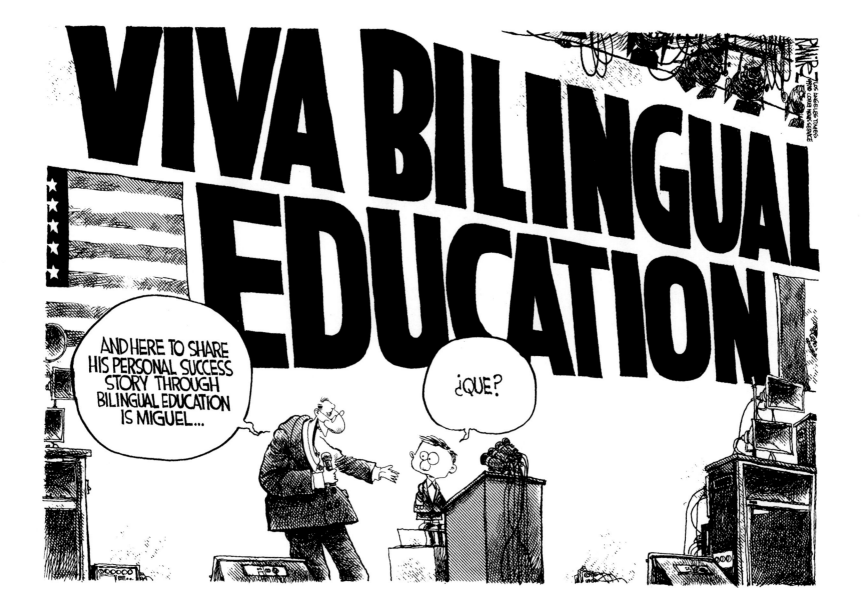

~71~

~72~

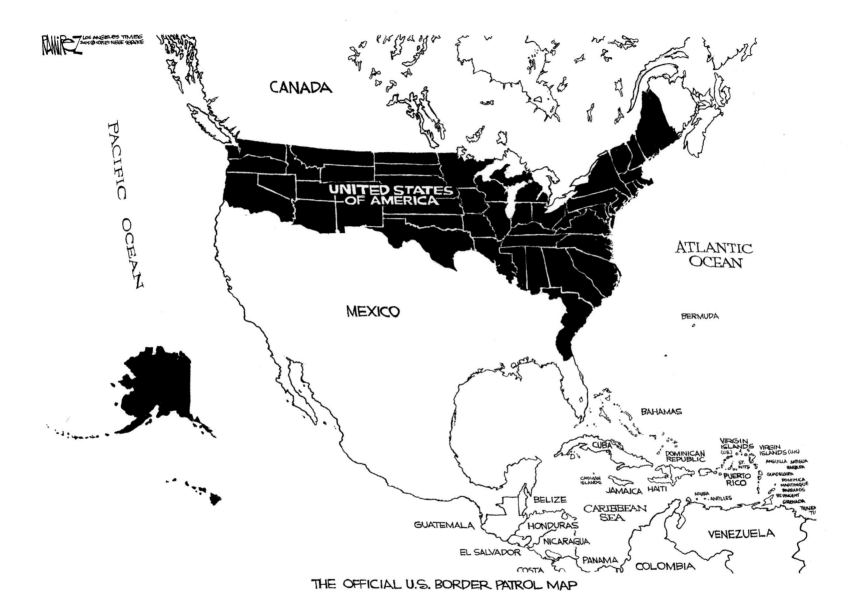

THE OFFICIAL U.S. BORDER PATROL MAP

BODY
ARMOR?

CHECK.

FLAK
VEST?

CHECK.

DECONTAMINATION
KIT?

CHECK.

COMBAT
BOOTS?

CHECK.

KEVLAR
HELMET?

CHECK.

GOOD LUCK
WITH THE
CONFIRMATION,
JUDGE ROBERTS.

THANK
YOU.

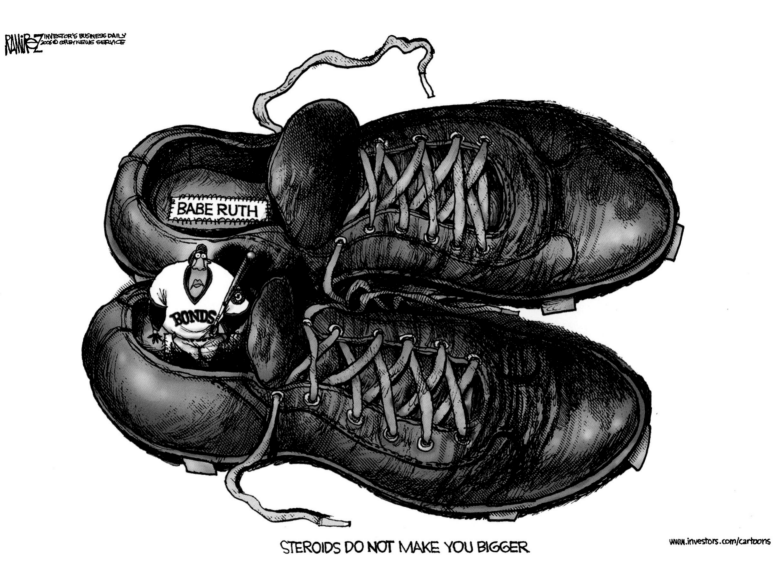

STEROIDS DO NOT MAKE YOU BIGGER

www.investors.com/cartoons

~80~

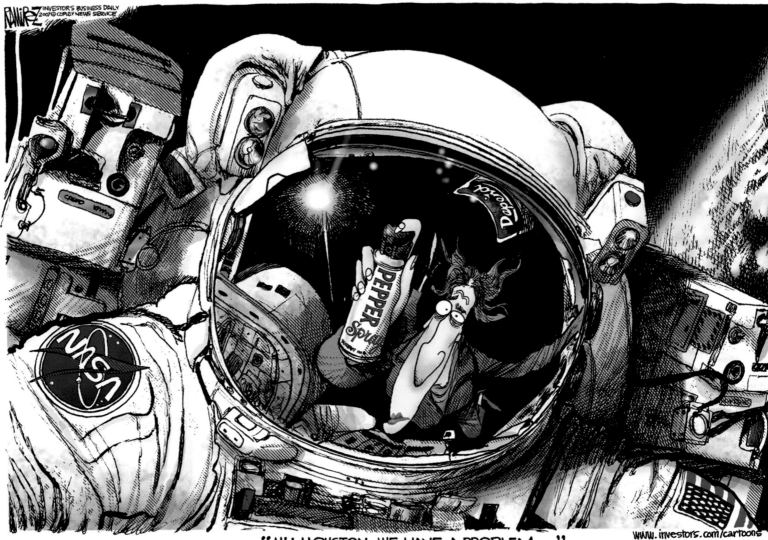

"UH HOUSTON, WE HAVE A PROBLEM...."

INQUISITION

"YOU DARE CHALLENGE GLOBAL WARMING WITH SCIENTIFIC DEBATE?"

"WE ARE ANTICIPATING ANOTHER 8-12 INCHES OF GLOBAL WARMING TODAY."

Baseball

BLINDERS

www.IBDeditorials.com/cartoons

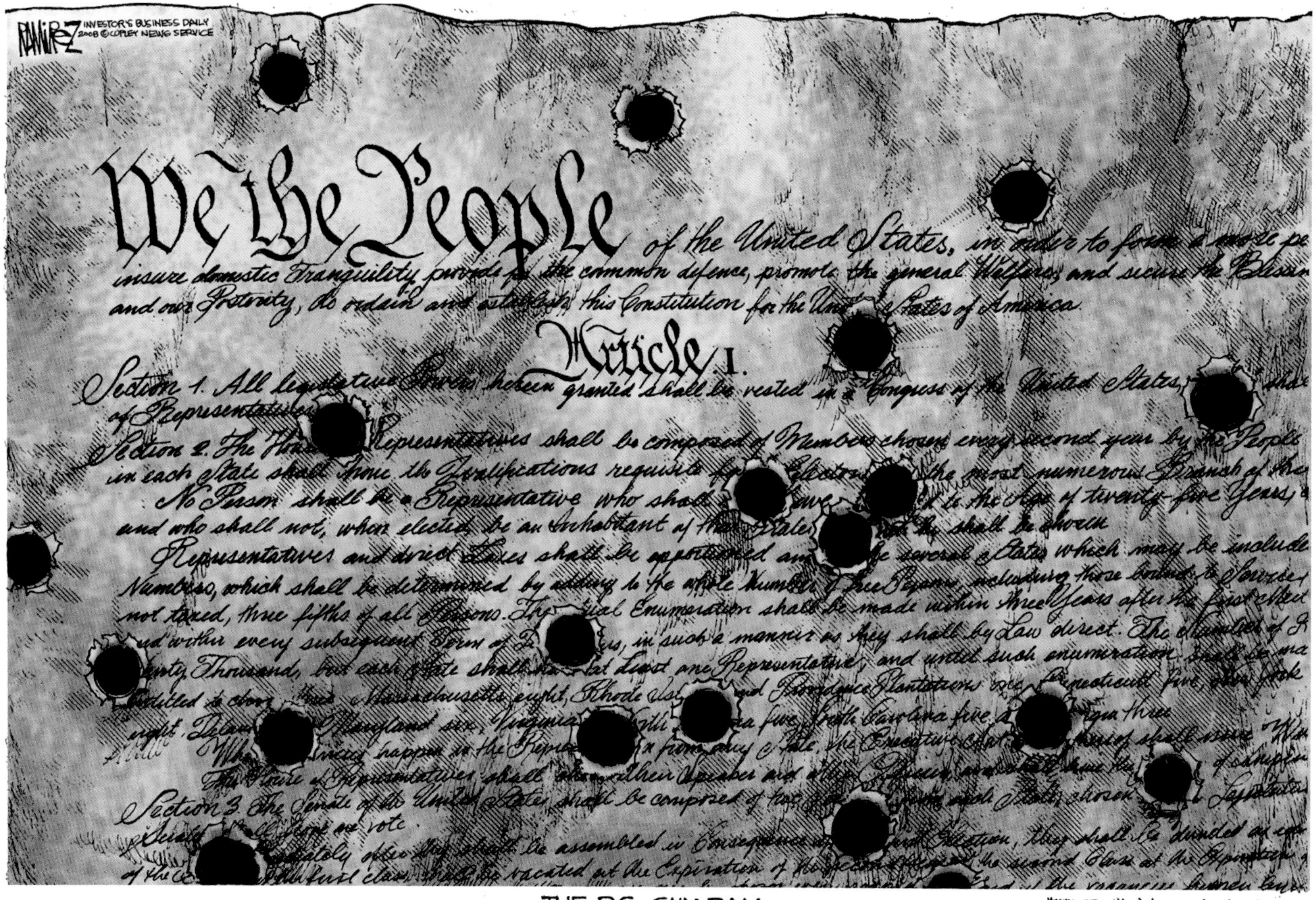

THE D.C. GUN BAN

www.ibdeditorials.com/cartoons

ECONOMICS

The business of America is business.

—Calvin Coolidge

~91~

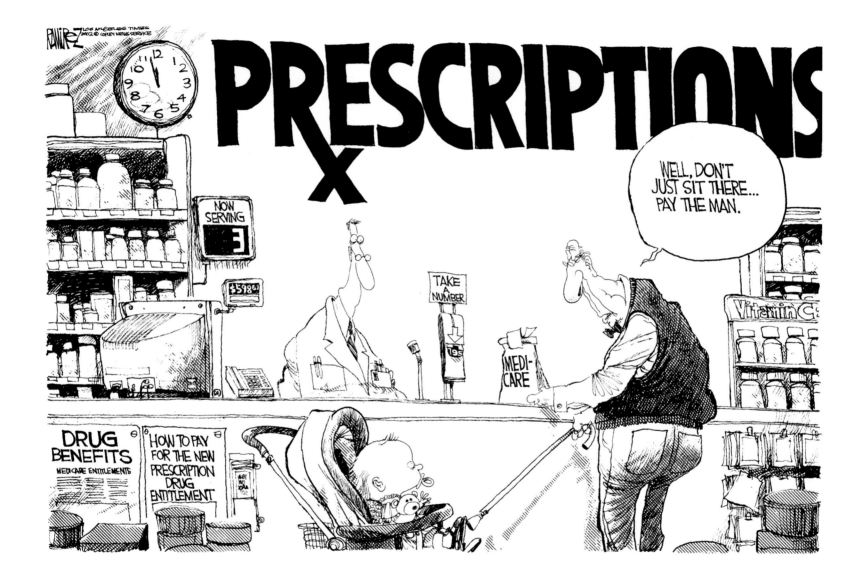

THE REAL ESTATE BUBBLE

QUALITY IS JOB 1

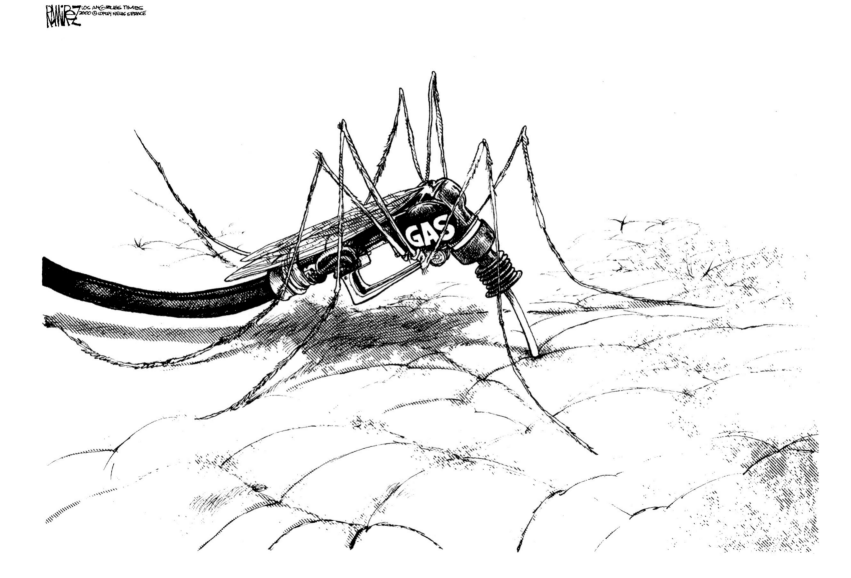

~100~

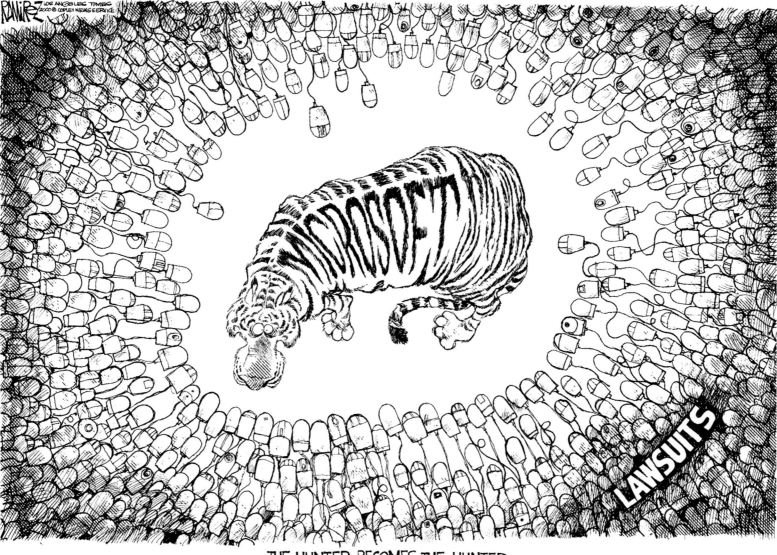

THE HUNTER BECOMES THE HUNTED.

DAY TRADING

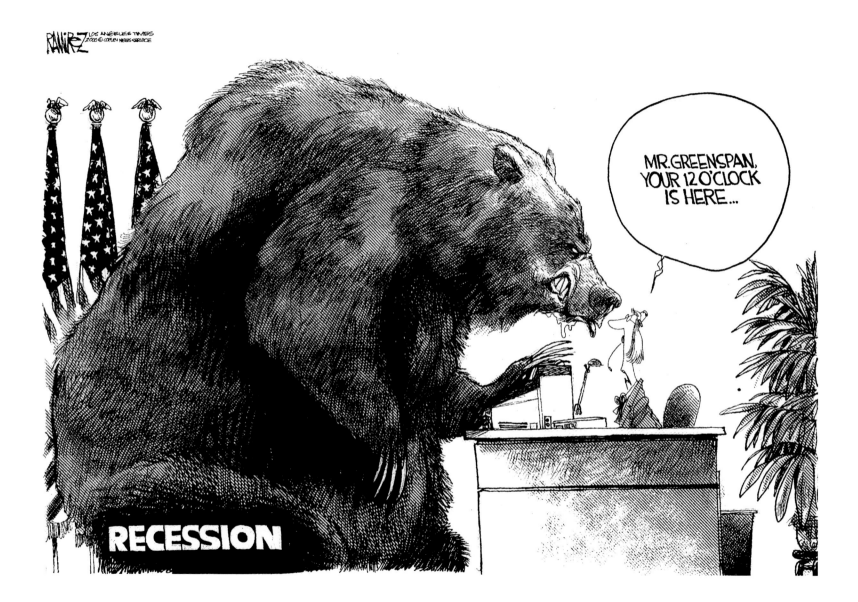

~104~

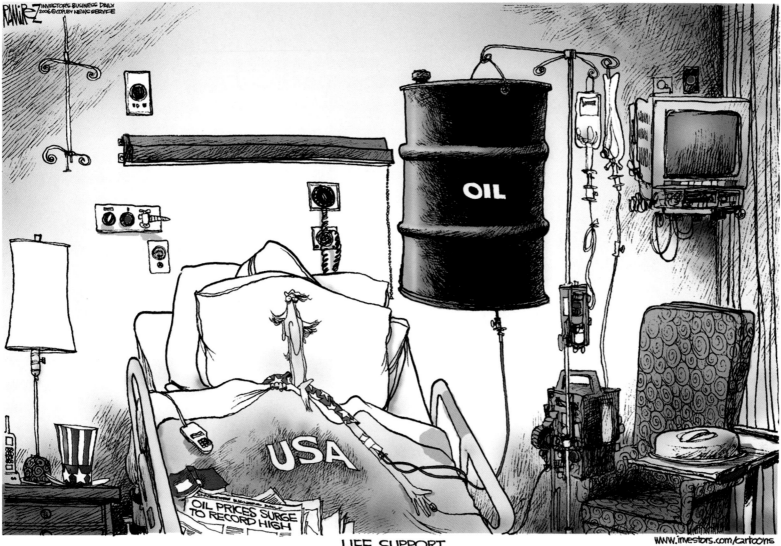

LIFE SUPPORT

~108~

~110~

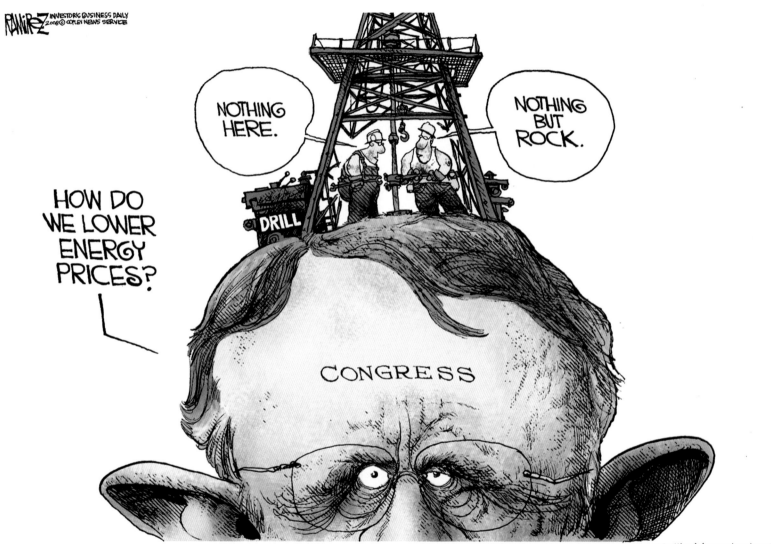

~114~

POLITICS

Government is not reason; it is not eloquence; it is force! Like fire, it is a dangerous servant and a fearful master.

—George Washington

THE STAIN

THE JERK

CONTEMPT

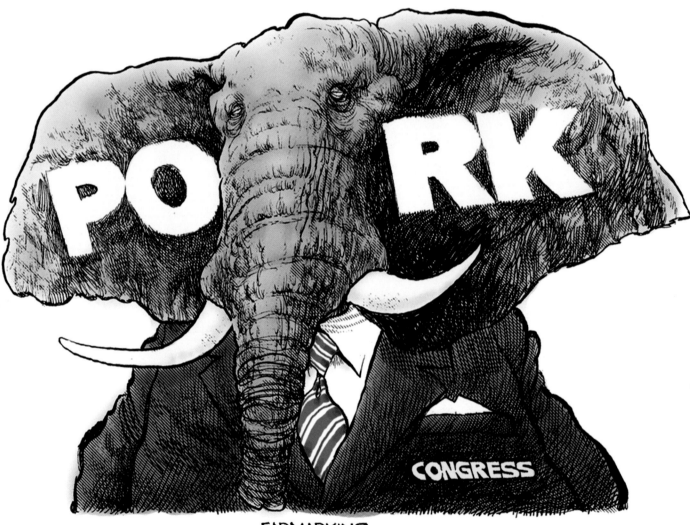

EARMARKING

~127~

~128~

"AND IT SAYS IF YOU DON'T COPY THIS AND SEND THIS TO TEN U.N. SECURITY COUNCIL MEMBERS BAD THINGS WILL HAPPEN TO YOU...."

AIR FORCE THREE

~133~

WHAT WE DID THIS SUMMER
by
Congress

The end.

www.IBDeditorials.com/kartoons

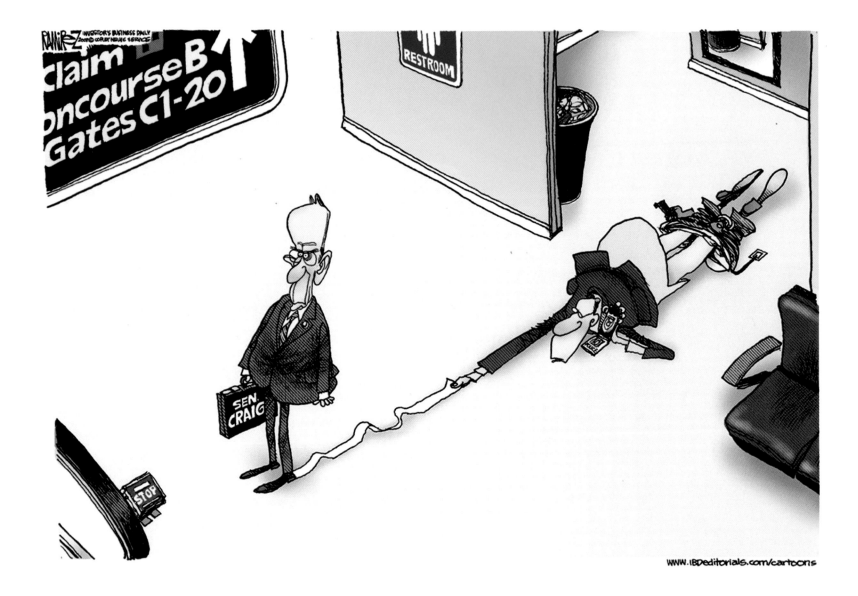

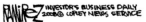

IT'S NOT LIKE I WAS HAVING SEX IN THE OVAL OFFICE.

JOHN F. KENNEDY

IT'S NOT LIKE I WAS SOLICITING SOME GUY IN THE MEN'S BATHROOM.

BILL CLINTON

IT'S NOT LIKE I WAS HAVING AN AFFAIR WITH A MALE AIDE.

LARRY CRAIG

IT'S NOT LIKE I WAS PAYING FOR A HOOKER.

JAMES McGREEVEY

IT'S NOT LIKE I WAS SNORTING COCAINE OR SMOKING DOPE.

ELIOT SPITZER

IT'S NOT LIKE I WAS OBSTRUCTING JUSTICE OR COMMITTING PERJURY.

DAVID PATERSON

THE EVOLUTION OF MORALITY IN POLITICS

www.IBDeditorials.com/cartoons

~137~

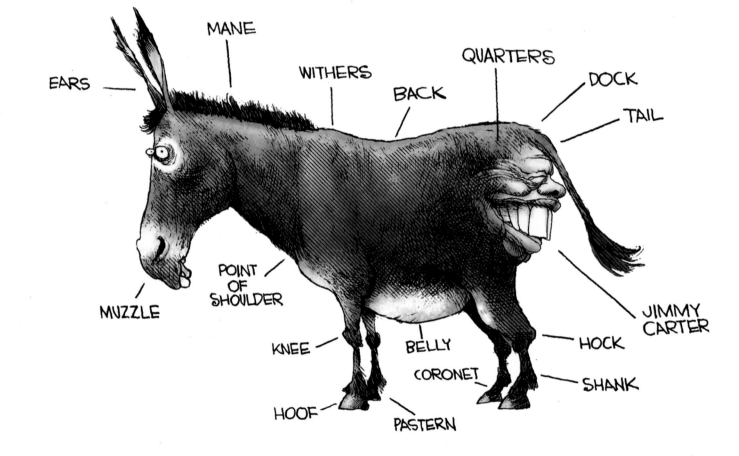

ELECTIONS

Nothing brings out the lower traits of human nature like office seeking.

—Rutherford B. Hayes

THE PARTING OF THE GOP

THE MANY POSITIONS OF JOHN KERRY

"DON'T WORRY, I HAVE EXPERIENCE. I'M NOT A SURGEON, BUT I WAS MARRIED TO ONE FOR EIGHT YEARS."

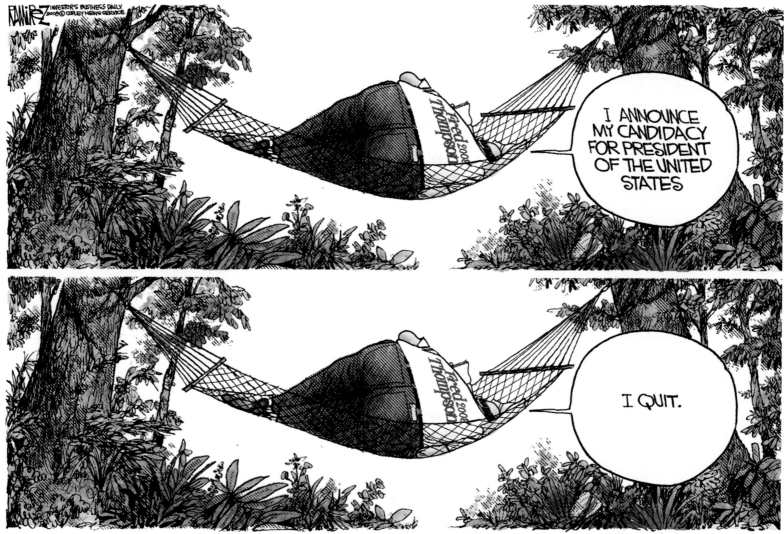

~153~

THE EMPEROR'S OLD CLOTHES

AND THERE HE SLEPT FOR TWENTY YEARS.

www.IBDeditorials.com/cartoons

OBAMA'S RHETORIC   OBAMA'S POLICIES

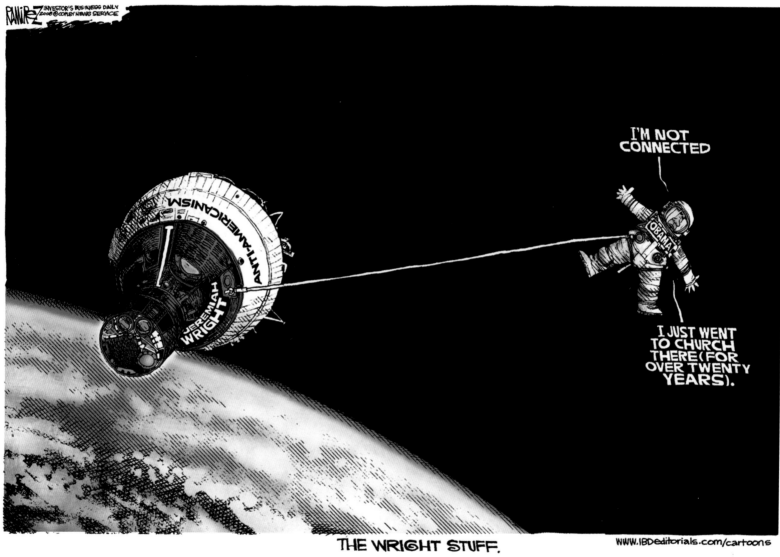

THE WRIGHT STUFF.

THE McCAIN MUTINY

www.IBDeditorials.com/cartoons

WORLD AFFAIRS

We are a nation that has a government—not the other way around.
And that makes us special among the nations of the earth.

—Ronald Wilson Reagan

THE EUROPEAN INVASION

"YES ELIAN, SOMEDAY ALL THIS WILL BE YOURS..."

~168~

~170~

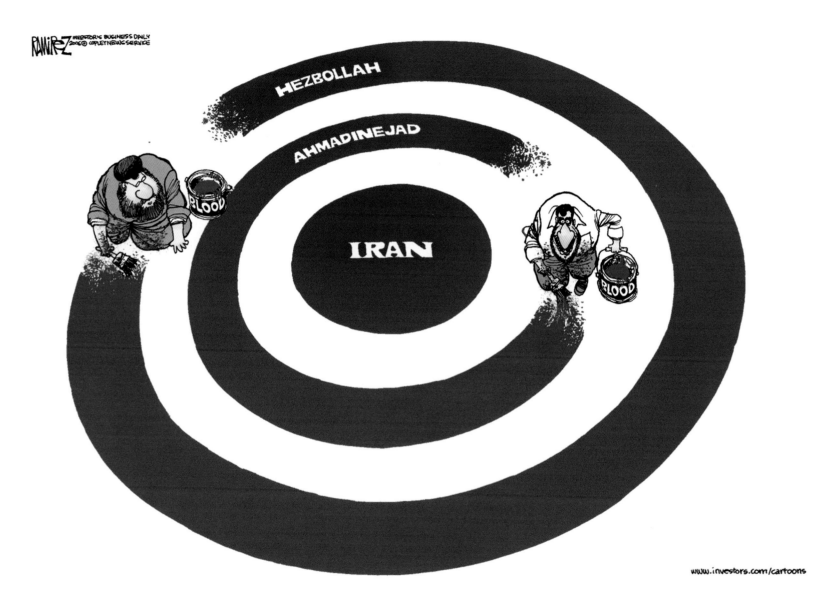

"WHAT'S THE MATTER, NEVER SEEN A *DOLPHIN* BEFORE?"

www.investors.com/cartoons

~182~

ENERGY

RUSSIA

CHINA EXECUTES FOOD AND DRUG CHIEF IN PRODUCT SAFETY CRISIS.

www.IBDeditorials.com/cartoons

~185~

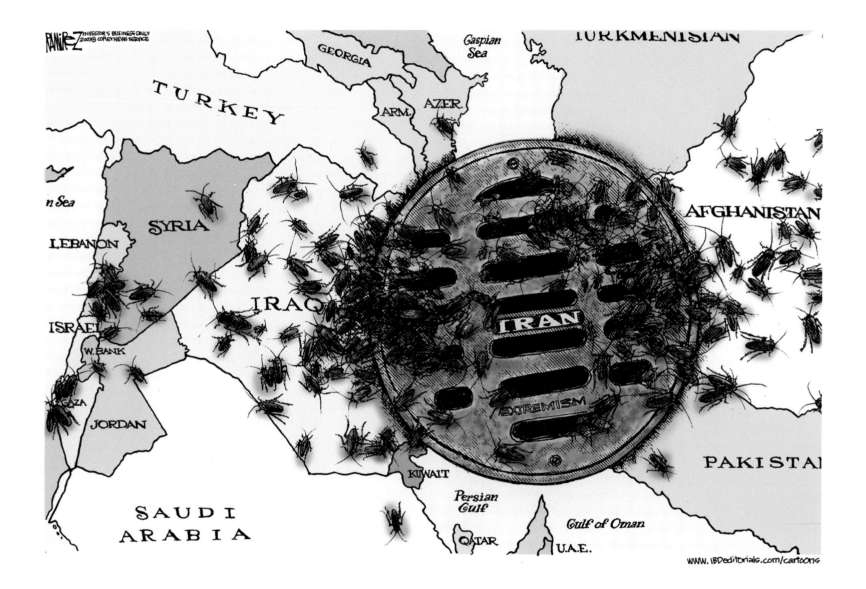

Beijing 2008

HUMAN RIGHTS

www.IBDeditorials.com/cartoons

~188~

THE MIDDLE EAST

If civilization is to survive, we must cultivate the science of human relationships—the ability of all peoples, of all kinds, to live together, in the same world at peace.

—Franklin D. Roosevelt

~191~

WORSHIPING THEIR GOD...

~192~

AN EYE FOR AN EYE FOR AN EYE FOR AN EYE FOR AN...

~197~

"AND THIS TIME IT VANISHED QUITE SLOWLY, BEGINNING WITH THE END OF THE TAIL, AND ENDING WITH THE GRIN, WHICH REMAINED SOME TIME AFTER THE REST OF IT HAD GONE..."

HAMAS

UNITY GOVERNMENT

SEPTEMBER 11

The price of freedom is eternal vigilance.

—Thomas Jefferson

"I GOT IT, I GOT IT..."

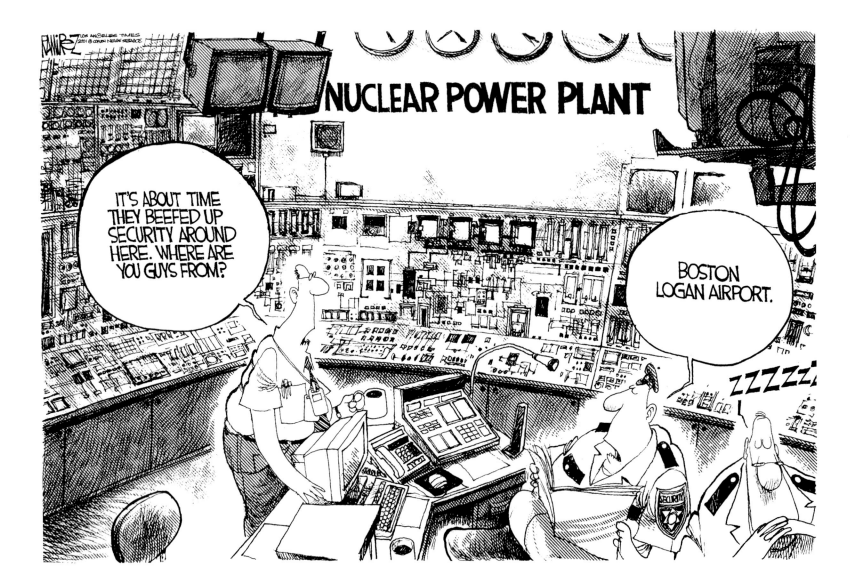

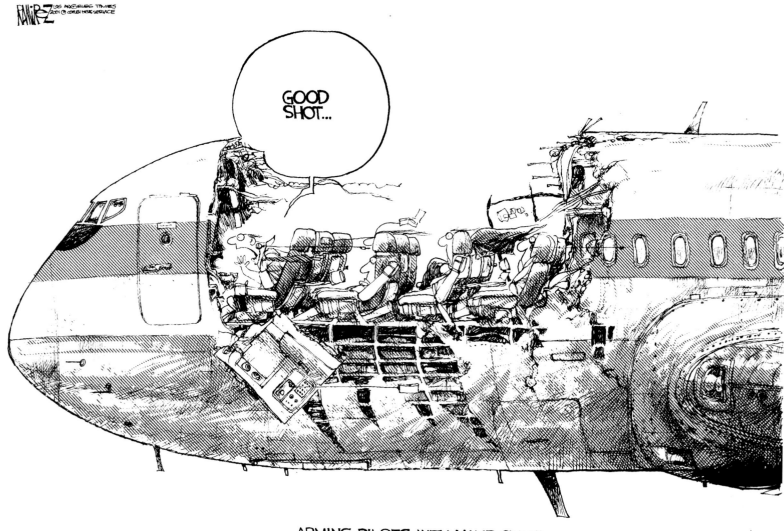

ARMING PILOTS WITH HAND GUNS...

THE STATE OF THE UNION

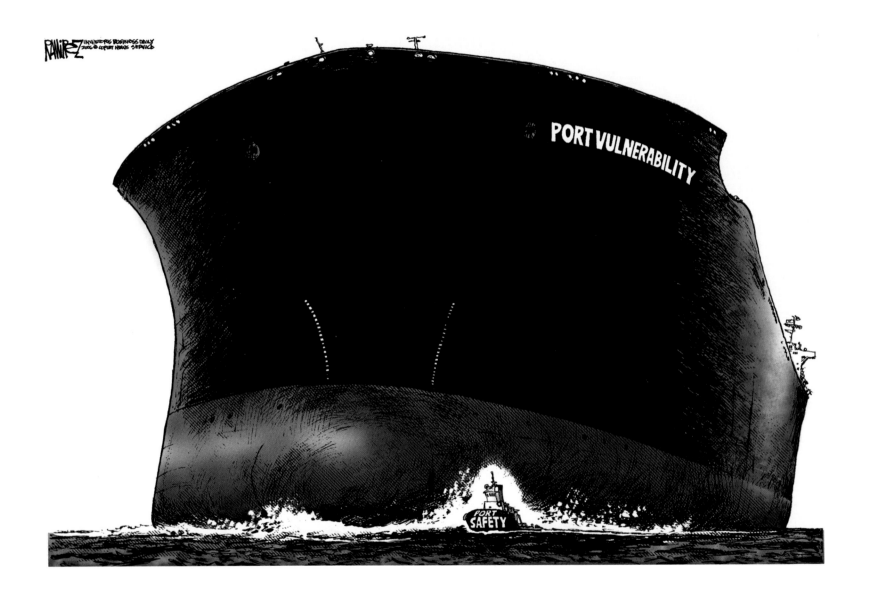

~214~

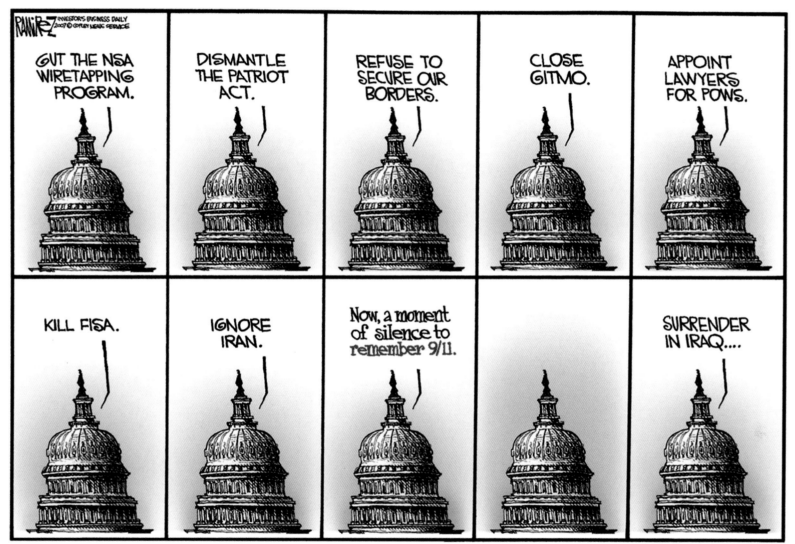

A Memorial Day Thank You

WAR

I never saw a pessimistic general win a battle.

—Dwight D. Eisenhower

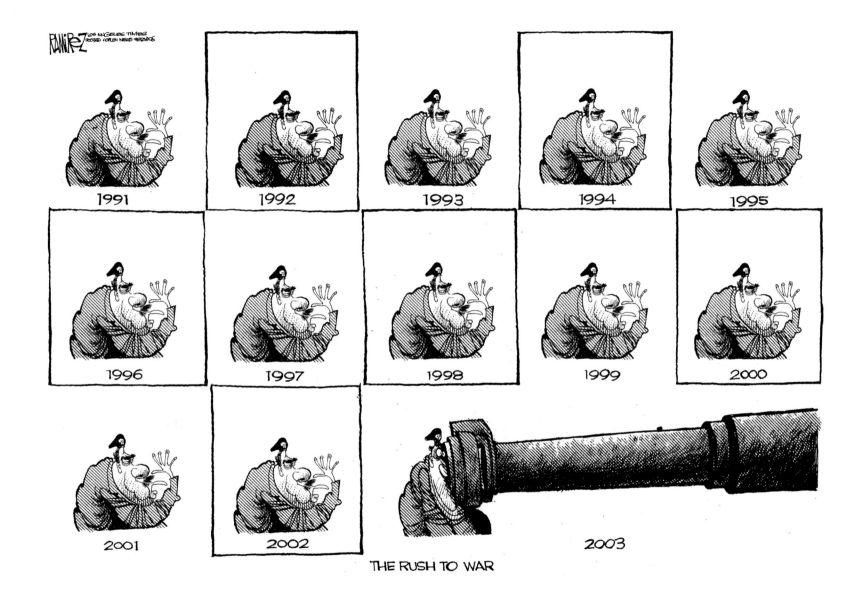

THE RUSH TO WAR

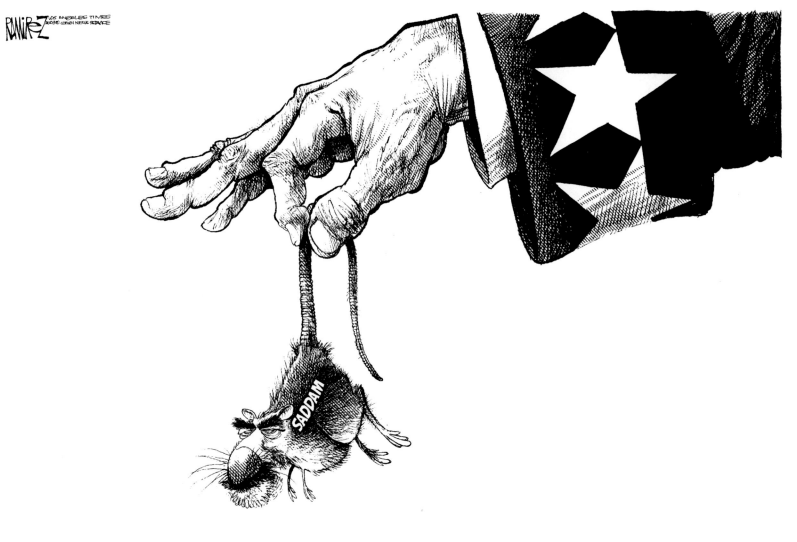

GOTCHA

THE STANDING OVATION

THE CASE AGAINST SADDAM

50,000 REASONS WHY THE WORLD IS BETTER OFF WITHOUT SADDAM HUSSEIN.

WAR ON TERROR

~229~

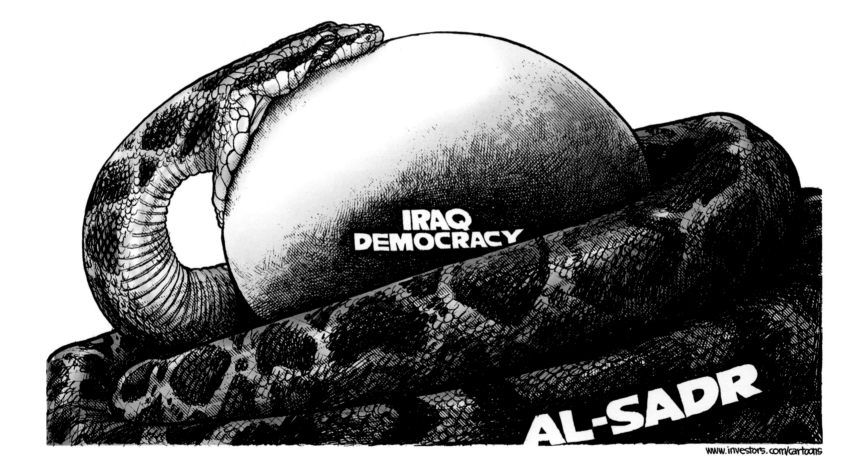

MATA HARRY REID

~233~

~234~

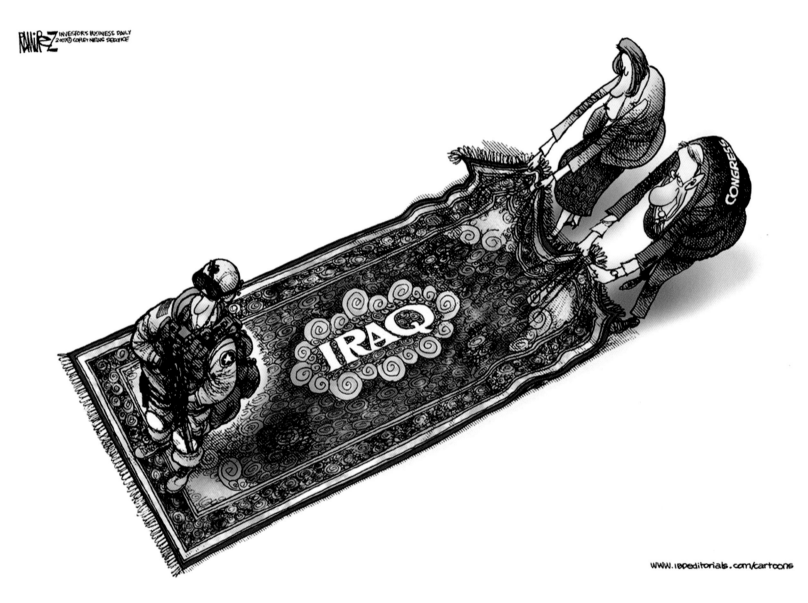

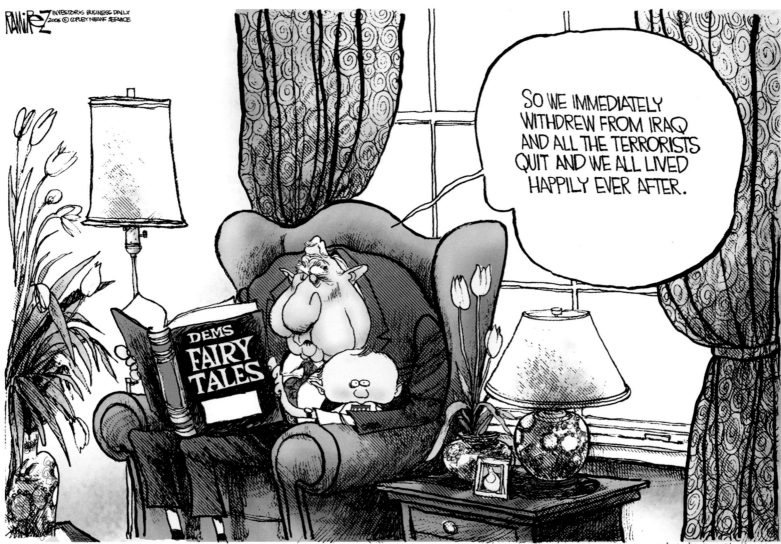

~237~

THE 1994 PULITZER COLLECTION

It depends on what the meaning of the word "is" is.

—William Jefferson Clinton

THE MORNING AFTER.

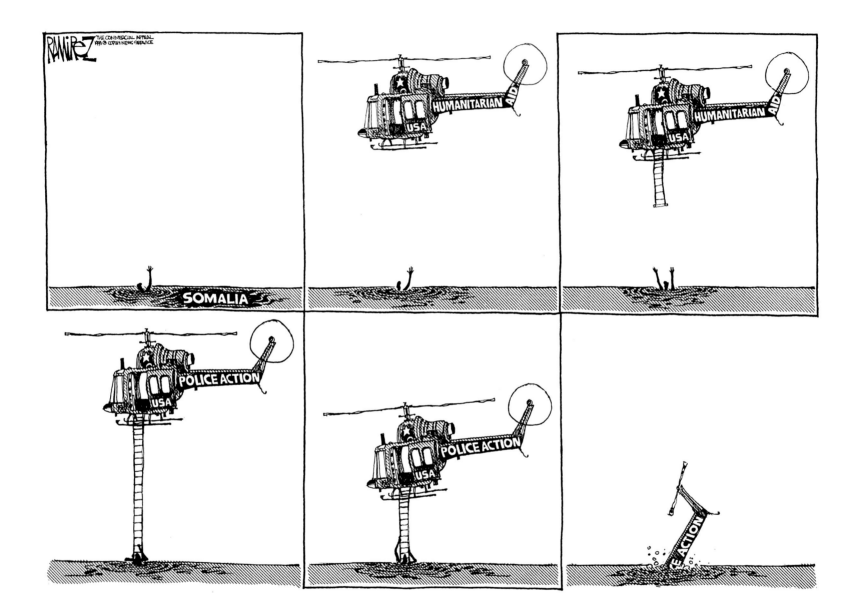

MEANWHILE, AT THE DENNY TRIAL...

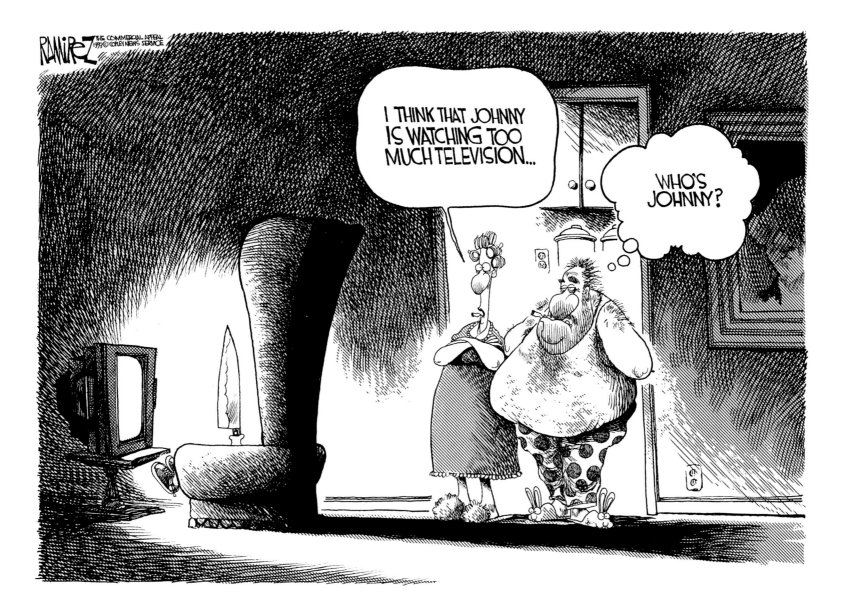

~253~

Humor is the only test of gravity, and gravity of humor; for a subject which will not bear raillery is suspicious, and a jest which will not bear serious examination is false wit.

—Aristotle

BACKWORD

My friend Michael Ramirez is one of a kind. As a man who knows a thing or two about satire, I can recognize a great satirist when I see one, and Michael Ramirez is among the best. When I met Michael a number of years ago in Hawaii, where we were both giving keynote speeches, I was honored to finally meet the man I had admired for so long. My wife, Hunter, and I have started our morning for years by opening the paper to the brilliance of our friend Michael Ramirez. It has always made our day.

Not only is Michael a great satirist and social commentator, he is a first-class pen-and-ink artist—a combination rarely found in editorial cartoonists. As you flipped through these pages, I hope you took the time to look at the art in addition to the commentary of the cartoons. Think of the artistry in the Winston Churchill/Harry Reid cartoon that features a detailed portrait of Churchill from his gold watch chain and his polka-dot bow tie to his timeworn face. It's a virtual photograph, although it isn't a photograph—it's a Michael Ramirez perfectly etched reproduction. In the cartoon, Churchill is uttering his famous World War II speech to the citizens of Great Britain facing Hitler in their darkest hour. "We shall fight on the beaches. We shall fight on the landing grounds. We shall fight in the fields and in the streets. We shall never surrender."

Next to Churchill, the liberal Nevada Senator Harry Reid shouts: "Run away!" Whatever your politics, the depiction of Churchill exhorting England to have the courage to stand firm juxtaposed to a wimpy Harry Reid saying, more or less, "Run for the exits!" is an exquisite piece of satire. The art is beautiful; the commentary, pointed.

It is no accident that Ramirez is a two-time Pulitzer Prize–winning editorial cartoonist. His work for *Investor's Business Daily* has been so outstanding it is challenging to pick a favorite. They are all sharp—sometimes wickedly so and sometimes heartbreakingly so. One imagines that "The Anchor" (the huge anchor marked "Couric" pulling on a chain connected to a *Titanic*-like CBS ship) was not terribly appreciated by Katie Couric or CBS chief Leslie Moonves. But the rest of us laughed. Devilishly sharp.

On the flip side, the cartoon of a starving third world child holding an empty plate in one hand and a skimpy ear of corn in the other, and a man in a business suit pulling the corn out of the child's hand while saying, "Excuse me, I'm going to need this to run my car" is beyond poignant at capturing the horrors of ethanol. Our so-called energy policy has real ramifications. Ramirez takes no prisoners in his criticism. That cartoon should make us all embarrassed and ashamed.

Ramirez mixes art and absurdity on a daily basis. One of my other favorite cartoons shows a beautifully drawn U.S. Capitol. The voice caption reads: "For the last time, if you don't tell us where you planted the nuclear device, we'll have no choice but to appoint a lawyer for you." Behind the Capitol, near the Washington Monument, a giant mushroom cloud rises in the sky. Brilliant satire.

Michael always calls things the way he sees them without regard to who might be offended. That's the way I have always operated, too. When I wrote and recorded "Green Chritma," an assault on the overcommercialization of Christmas, a number of years back, big business was not pleased. Madison Avenue attacked me, and even the executives at Capitol Records had their doubts. I have often said, "My records are not released—they escape." Thank God we have Michael Ramirez, whose magnificent work "escapes"

into newspapers and online, so that the whole world can laugh at the genius of a man who is likely well on his way to his third Pulitzer. The bad news for us is that politicians and government will continue to do incredibly stupid things; the good news for Michael is that he will no doubt find great material to work with in the years to come. We can all take some comfort in having Michael Ramirez around to skewer the idiocy, ignorance, tyranny, and absurdities of our world.

—**Stan Freberg**
Los Angeles, California